GW00658896

Saints and Patrons

Christian names for
Baptism & Confirmation

by
Joanna Bogle

*All booklets are published thanks to the
generous support of the members of the
Catholic Truth Society*

CATHOLIC TRUTH SOCIETY
PUBLISHERS TO THE HOLY SEE

Contents

The tradition of naming 3

Saints' names for girls 9

Saints' names for boys 33

The tradition of naming

When a child is baptised, the parents choose a name. Often it will be linked with a family tradition – perhaps a person or even a place that the family has known and loved, a character from a book or a film, or simply a well-known public personality. But Baptism is a Sacrament. The essential thing about the name that is given when the priest says "I baptise you..." is that it must be Christian.

A baptismal name is important "because God knows each of us by name, that is, in our uniqueness as persons. In Baptism a Christian receives his or her own name in the Church. It should preferably be the name of a saint who might offer the baptised model of sanctity and an assurance of his or her intercession before God."(*Compendium of the Catechism of the Catholic Church*)

A child will often be given two or three names. This offers scope for honouring all sorts of things. In addition to choosing a saint's name, there could be a name honouring a Christian virtue such as Hope or Faith, or one of the fruits of the Holy Spirit such as Joy or Peace. There are also important names from the Old Testament such as Noah or Joshua or Rebecca.

In the very early Church the sacraments of Baptism and Confirmation were often administered together. Over time, as the Church grew and it became impossible for a Bishop to be present at every baptism, Confirmation came to be administered separately. It includes anointing with oil. The *Catechism of the Catholic Church* teaches that "By Confirmation, Christians, that is, those who are anointed, share more completely in the mission of Jesus Christ and the fullness of the Holy Spirit with which he is filled..." (CCC 1294). Confirmation "brings an increase and deepening of baptismal grace" (CCC 1302). Like Baptism, it is "given only once, for it too imprints on the soul an indelible spiritual mark, the 'character' which is the sign that Jesus Christ has marked a Christian with the seal of his Spirit by clothing him with power from on high so that he may be his witness." (CCC 1304).

It is traditional to take a new name at Confirmation, an addition to the name given at Baptism. This is an opportunity for the Confirmation candidate to choose a name that carries some personal significance.

This booklet offers some suggestions for names for Baptism and Confirmation. In modern Britain, Catholics are usually confirmed at about the age of ten or eleven, but of course the sacrament may be conferred earlier – and there are every year also many adult Confirmations. Whether a child, a teenager or an adult, the candidate can take time – and pleasure – in choosing a name that will hold real meaning and significance.

Considerations when choosing names

There will be all sorts of considerations when pondering a possible Confirmation name. You may like to commemorate a much-loved grandparent or other relation who has died, by sharing the same saint's name. You may want to make a special link with a saint whose life makes a particular link with yours – who lived in your town or district, or whose life involved problems and challenges similar to yours. Or there may be particular things that you admire – courage in the face of martyrdom, integrity in public service, heroic missionary work, or a dedicated priestly life.

There are saints whose lives are very well-known – they have virtually become household names. Most people have heard about St Peter, or St Andrew, and there are hero-martyrs such as St Thomas More, and popular 19th century saints such as St Bernadette of Lourdes, and St Thérèse of Lisieux. Other saints have slipped into history, and we know very little about them, except that they left behind a legend or an association with some small village.

You may want to use the English form of a saint's name, or you may find it sounds more interesting in its original form. For example, a famous French saint is Marguerite-Marie Alacoque, who through her visions and mystical experiences brought to the world the popular devotion to Christ's Sacred Heart which has been central in the Church ever since. She is known in English as Margaret-Mary, and other forms of this are Margery or Marjorie. And the name Margaret is itself very old – the original St Margaret was a martyr in the days of the pagan Roman Empire. The word itself means "pearl" and it has lots of variants including Maggie, Madge, Margie, Rita, Peggy, Greta, Gretchen, Margot and Megan. And a great English martyr-saint bears the name: Margaret Clitheroe, known as the "pearl of York".

The Church canonises new saints all the time. Pope John Paul II canonised a great number – more than all his predecessors had done down all the centuries. He did this to emphasise the central role of saints in the life of the Church – and to pay tribute to the huge variety of saints in the life of the Church – men and women from every walk of life, living in all sorts of circumstances, enduring all sorts of trials, tackling all sorts of challenges. Some saints were priests, some were missionaries, some were martyrs. Some were married people raising families. Some were active in public life – St Thomas More was Lord Chancellor of England, Edward the Confessor was a King – while some lived quiet humble lives in convents or monasteries.

Several saints with the same name

Because there are several saints with the same name, you may decide to choose a saint's surname – like "Newman" for John Henry Newman (the great English priest, writer, and Cardinal of the 19th century whose writings are still hugely important today) or "Campion" for St Edmund Campion (the heroic English martyr from the 16th century, who was tortured in the Tower of London and died at Tyburn). Or you may like to choose a name that has been carried by many saints and while having one as your special patron you feel a connection with the others. St Peter was the first Pope and Christ gave him "the keys of the kingdom of Heaven" (Mt 1:19), making him the "rock" on which the Church was established. His name has been carried by other saints and heroes, like St Peter Claver (1580-1654) who worked to help suffering African slaves in Spanish South America.

Adapt a saint's name

You may also like to adapt a saint's name in some way – for example, a girl may wish to feminise the name of a male saint, hence Francesca for St Francis, or Michaela for St Michael. And abbreviations can sometimes be appropriate – for example, Bernadette was originally a diminutive for Bernarde. Sometimes a place-name has become so identified with a saint that it can work as a name in its own right – Lourdes, for example. If you wanted to be unusual, you might decide to choose a place-name such as Tyburn honouring the English martyrs, or Lincoln to honour St Hugh who was Bishop there and risked his life saving Jews from a mob of thugs, or Bethany where Martha and Mary welcomed Christ into their home, or Assisi where St Francis lived.

A patron saint

Choosing a patron saint is something valuable. It is important to understand what the Church teaches about saints, and how they can help us by their prayers in Heaven. We speak of the "communion of saints", and affirm our belief in it every time we say the Creed at Mass. There is a real unity, through the Church, with all who have died in the Faith of Christ and who are with him in glory.

A patron saint is not just someone whose example we can follow and whose life inspires us: he or she is someone in Heaven who can intercede for us and help us. St Thérèse of Lisieux famously said "I want to spend my heaven doing good on earth."

Saints' names for girls

Abigail, the name means "one who brings joy to her father", is an Old Testament name: she was the wife of King David (see the Book of Samuel). The Irish version of this name is sometimes said to be **Gobnait**, and there was a saint of that name who founded churches at Dunquin in Co Kerry and Dungarvan in Co Waterford and a monastery at Ballyvourney, Co Cork, with St Abban. St Gobnait kept illness at bay by consecrating the ground all around the monastery. She kept bees and is the patron saint of beekeepers.

Agatha (d. c.251) was a martyr of the early Church, born in Sicily, where she is still very much celebrated as a local saint. She is one of seven women saints listed in the Canon of the Mass, and died because, legend says, she refused the immoral advances of a pagan ruler, undergoing various grim tortures before her final execution.

Amelia/Amalia (Millie/Mia) – the name means "work" or "industry". St **Amelia** (741-772) was born into a noble family and wanted to become a nun. But the King's son, Charles – later to be known as the great ruler

Charlemagne – wanted to marry her and begged her to be his bride. It is said that once, in trying to force her to come with him, he broke her arm. Finally he accepted that she wanted to dedicate her life to Christ alone. The arm was miraculously healed, and she went on to found a great church at Temse on the river Schelde. She is sometimes known as St **Amalberga**.

Anastasia (early 4th century) was a martyr in the reign of the Emperor Diocletian. Her name means "Resurrection", and she is listed in the Canon of the Mass . She is much honoured in the Eastern (Orthodox and Greek Catholic) Church where she is known as the "great martyr".

Anne-Marie/Marianne/Marian There are many versions of this name, linking together Our Lady and her mother, St Anne. The Scriptures do not give us the name of Mary's mother, but tradition has long named her as **Anne**, which is the same name as **Hannah** in the Old Testament.

Aurelia (d.1027) was an Austrian princess, who renounced marriage because she wanted to dedicate herself wholly to God. She became a hermit, living in seclusion in a Benedictine abbey near Salzburg, and was forgotten by her family and the wider world. Her holiness and life of prayer were later made known by the local Bishop, St Wolfgang of Regensburg.

Bakhita (c.1869-1947) Josephine Bakhita was born in Africa, captured by slave traders while still a small child, and endured terrible sufferings at the hands of various owners before finally passing into the hands of an Italian family who treated her kindly and introduced her to an order of nuns. After a legal case had established that she could not be regarded as a slave as slavery was illegal in Italy, she became a nun influencing many by her kindness, dedication to prayer, and desire to spread the Gospel. She is patron saint of Sudan and invoked by all who suffer injustice or modern forms of slavery.

Barbara (dates uncertain, possibly early 4th century) was a martyr of the early Church. Legend says she was locked up in a tower by her father, a pagan, while he went away on a long journey. On his return, discovering that she had meanwhile become a Christian and had turned the tower into a place of prayer with three windows to honour the Trinity, he killed her with his sword. At the moment he did so, he was struck dead by lightning. St Barbara (feast day December 4th) is the patron of thunderstorms.

Birgitta/Bridget of Sweden (1303-1373) was a noblewoman, related to the royal family and married to the governor of Uppland, by whom she had eight children. She was a mystic, and her visions and her charitable works had a profound influence on the royal court and subsequently on the whole of Sweden. Later as a widow she founded the religious order which bears her name, travelled to Rome where she established a religious house, and also made a pilgrimage to Jerusalem. She is one of the patron saints of Europe. St **Bridget (Bride/Bridie)** (c.451-525) of Kildare is one of Ireland's patron saints and was a nun, founder of several religious communities, known for her care for the poor and her kindliness and sanctity. She is sometimes called "the Mary of the Gael" and as Abbess of Kildare played a major role in establishing Christianity in Ireland.

Carol   (Carola/Caroline/Carolyn/Charlotte/Carlotta) are all feminine forms of the male name Charles or Karl. These names can commemorate a number of saints, including Charles Borromeo, Bl. Karl von Habsburg, and Karol Wojtyła (better known as Bl. John Paul). St **Caroline Gerhardinger** founded the School Sisters of Notre Dame in Bavaria in the 19th century and opened up education for large numbers of girls.

Catherine (Cathy/Katie/Kate/Kathryn/Katherine/ Catriona) (4th century) was a martyr of the early Church, traditionally said to have been tortured by being crushed on a spiked wheel (hence the Catherine Wheel firework). **Catherine of Siena** (1347-1380) was a mystic and reformer whose dedication to the Church brought Pope Gregory XI back to Rome from exile in Avignon. Her writings continue to inspire people today and she is a Doctor of the Church. **Catherine Labouré** (1806-1876) was a Daughter of Charity nun whose visions of Our Lady resulted in the Miraculous Medal, one of the most popular of all devotions in the Church. **Kateri** (Catherine) **Tekakwitha** (1656-1680) is known as "the lily of the Mohawks". She was born into the Mohawk Indian tribe and orphaned at the age of six in a smallpox epidemic which also left her with a badly pockmarked face and poor eyesight. She became a Christian despite ferocious opposition, and developed a great veneration for the Eucharist, often praying outside the small mission church all night to be able to greet Christ as soon as it opened in the morning. She is a patron saint of teenage chastity.

Cecily/Cecilia (3rd century) was a martyr in the Roman Empire, who died in Rome or possibly in Sicily. Legend says she was a married woman, of a noble Roman family, and her husband and brother-in-law were also both martyred. She is said to have been suffocated in a heated room of steam. She is patron saint of music because she is aid to have sung joyously on her way to death. There has been a church in her honour in Rome since the 5th century.

Christina/Christine (dates unknown, possibly 4th century). The name means "a young girl who is a follower of Christ". There was a martyr named Christina who died in one of the persecutions in the Roman Empire. She was buried at Bolsena in Italy. Later a number of legends came to be written about her, focussing on her courage.

Claire/Clare/Chiara (1194-1253) was one of the first followers of St Francis of Assisi. She founded an Order of nuns following the Franciscan rule, which became known as the Poor Clares and still flourishes today. An enclosed, austere order, its members focus on prayer and a simple, humble, hard-working life.

Diana (1201-1236). This was the name given by the pagan Ephesians to their goddess. But there is also a Blessed Diana, who was a Dominican nun in the 13th century. She took vows despite the violent opposition of her family – who once kidnapped her and took her home again – and eventually founded a great abbey dedicated to St Agnes.

Dominica is the feminine form of Dominic. There was also a St Dominica (d. 4th century) who was a martyr of the early Church about whom little is known. Blessed **Dominica Ongata** (d.1622) was a Japanese martyr who was beheaded in one of the great persecutions of the faith in that country: along with a number of other Japanese, she was converted following the arrival in Japan of the Jesuit Bl. Charles Spinola. When the authorities realised how strong the Church was becoming, there was a great persecution in which many Christians were tortured and executed.

Dorothy/Dorothea/Dora (d.c.311) was a virgin martyr of the early Church. It is said that on her way to execution, she was mocked by a young man who told her to send him some fruits from the heavenly garden where she had said she would soon be living. As she knelt for beheading, three fresh roses and three apples suddenly appeared beside her. These were sent to the young man, who later converted and is honoured as St Theophilus.

Edith/Eadgyth (961-984) of Kemsing was an Anglo-Saxon princess, an illegitimate daughter of King Edgar. She refused the crown of England, preferring to be a nun and care for the poor. She looked after leper children and the blind in Kemsing in Kent where she is still commemorated. **Edith Stein** (1891-1942) born into a devout Jewish family in Prussia, studied philosophy and became known as a writer and teacher. She became a Catholic and joined the Carmelites taking the name Teresa Benedicta of the Cross. She was arrested as a Jew by the Nazis in World War II and murdered in Auschwitz, one of the six million Jews killed in the Holocaust. She is a patron saint of Europe.

Elizabeth (Bess/Bessie/Beth/Betty/Lisbeth/Libby/Lizzie/Elspeth/Isobel) was a cousin of Mary, and mother of John the Baptist. Immediately after the Annunciation, Mary went to visit Elizabeth, who greeted her with words that we still use in the *Hail Mary*: "Blessed art thou among women, and blessed is the fruit of thy womb". Down the centuries, there have been many saints named after her, notably **Elizabeth of Hungary** (1207-1231), who married Ludwig of Thuringia and became known for her holiness and her care for the poor. When Ludwig went to the Crusades, she took charge of public affairs with great skill, in addition to founding a new hospital and organising relief for victims of famine. After his death she took vows of poverty and died in a hospice she had founded at Marburg. See also **Isabel/Isabella**.

Emma (980-1045) was born into a noble family, and brought up at the royal court of Bamberg. She married Count Wilhelm of Friesach. They had two sons who were tragically murdered, and later William himself died. Emma devoted herself entirely to the service of the poor, and founded ten churches and also a monastery. She is honoured at the cathedral in Gurk in Austria where she is buried.

Emerentiana (early 4th century) was another Roman martyr. Legend makes her the daughter of the nurse of St Agnes. After Agnes was martyred, Emerentiana went to pray at St Agnes's tomb. She was caught there by a pagan mob and was stoned to death: she is sometimes depicted surrounded by stones.

Emily (Emelina/Emiliana) - the name may be of the same root as **Amelia** but this is not certain. St **Emily de Rodat** (1787-1852) became a nun in France in the early 19th century but was not satisfied with a life of contemplation – she wanted to be active in serving the poor and needy. With three other nuns, she founded the Congregation of the Holy Family and in due course opened homes for orphans, for impoverished women, and for the elderly. By the time she died, there were nearly 40 such homes across France.

Endellion/Endelienta (dates unknown, 6th century) is said to have been a daughter of the Cornish king Brychan, and to have evangelised the area of Cornwall around the village that now bears her name.

Etheldreda (Audrey) (630-679) was an Anglo-Saxon princess, the daughter of King Ana of East Anglia. She wanted to be a nun, but was obliged for reasons of state to marry the king of a neighbouring kingdom. She only did this on condition of remaining a virgin. When he sought to break this agreement she fled to a monastery. In due course she became famed as a great abbess of holiness and wisdom, building a great church at Ely, and living in personal austerity while helping the local people in times of trouble or distress.

Fabiola (d.399) was a young Roman woman of some wealth and position, who divorced her first husband, married a second and then later became a Christian and renounced her comfortable life to dedicate herself to the service of the poor and sick. She was a student of St Jerome, travelled to Bethlehem, and in her final years founded a hospice for pilgrims in Rome.

Faith is one of the three Cardinal Virtues, the others being **Hope** and **Charity** and all are very suitable as Confirmation names along with other virtues such as **Mercy**, or **Patience**. There was a St **Faith** or **Foy** (d.c.297) who was an early Christian martyr, associated with Aquitaine in France, but little seems to be known about her.

Faustina (1905-1938) was a Polish nun whose visions of Christ gave the Church a devotion to the Divine Mercy that has become widely popular. St Faustina saw Christ with rays of red and white light pouring out from his heart, and pictures of this are now in Catholic homes and churches and schools around the world with the simple prayer "Jesus, I trust in you".

Felicity (d.203) – the name means "joy" - was a young married slave-woman, who was expecting a baby when she was arrested for being a Christian. She was arrested along with her employer, Perpetua, who had recently had a baby. They suffered martyrdom at Carthage in North Africa, then part of the Roman Empire, and they share a feast-day on March 7th.

Francesca/Frances (Francie/Frankie) is the feminine form of **Francis**. See below. See also St Jane Frances de Chantal.

Frideswide (c.650-735) is the patron saint of the city of Oxford. She is said to have been of royal birth, the daughter of an Anglo-Saxon king. Refusing an offer of marriage to a prince, she became a hermit and eventually established a religious community which flourished.

Gemma means "precious jewel" (hence our English word "gem"). St **Gemma Galgani** (1878-1903) was a mystic, who had a great devotion to Christ's suffering on Calvary. Orphaned at the age of 18, she shared with her aunt the care of younger siblings, while working as a housekeeper for a local family. She had visions of Christ and of Mary, and endured much physical suffering, dying of tuberculosis.

Geneviève (419-502) is the patron saint of Paris. She is said to have launched a great crusade of personal prayer that saved the city from being sacked by Attila the Hun and his troops. Later, when the city was again besieged, this time by the Frankish invader Childeric, she acted as spokesman for the city's people, negotiating with Childeric and begging for the release of prisoners.

Hedwig (1174-1243) born in Bavaria, married the Duke of Silesia and spent much of her married life involved with attempts at peace negotiations in the various territorial wars in her husband's lands. But both she and her husband were benefactors of the Church, founded monasteries, helped the poor, promoted agriculture and sought to foster justice for all the territories they ruled. Hedwig identified herself with the poor and went barefoot, even in winter – it was said that one day when urged to wear shoes she put them on her hands instead of on her feet. The Cathedral in Berlin is dedicated to her.

Helen/Helena/Eleanor/Ellen (c.248-330) was the mother of the Roman emperor Constantine, who ended the persecution of Christians in the Empire. Tradition makes her a Briton. She became a Christian late in life, and devoted her time to caring for the poor and homeless. She went on a pilgrimage to the Holy Land and there she found pieces of the Cross on which Christ died and brought them back to Rome as relics.

Henrietta/Harriet: feminine form of Henry.

Hilda (614-680) founded the abbey at Whitby, where the famous Synod of Whitby was held, which sought to reconcile the Irish and Anglo-Saxon Christian rites and customs. The abbey was a centre of literature and learning and Hilda was a leading figure in the Church whose wisdom was sought by kings and bishops.

Hildegard (1098-1179) was a nun who was a mystic and a writer, an artist, musician, philosopher and academic, with a wide knowledge of medicine. Her writings are still widely studied today and she is the patron saint of women scholars.

Irene (d.304) – the name means "peace". There was a martyr of this name in the early 4th century at Thessalonika, said to have been one of three sisters brought before the local governor for refusing the renounce their Christian faith. Irene was a scholar who kept Christian books. She refused to pay honour to the pagan gods and was burned alive.

Isabel/Isabella of Portugal (1271-1336) was of the Spanish Royal family, Aragon, one of the most powerful families in Europe. She married King Denis of Portugal and caused some controversy by holding firmly to her religious beliefs and many works of charity. She prayed the Divine Office daily, fasted, and worked on a range of projects for the poor and needy. Her life was not easy because of family politics and civil war and she played a dramatic and ultimately successful role in peacemaking between her husband and her son – once actually intervening between them on the battlefield. In her widowhood, she founded various convents and continued with charitable works, especially famine relief and the education of young girls.

Ita also known as **Deidre** (d.570) was of a noble family, and founded a convent in County Limerick. She established a school at Killeedy, where one of the pupils was St Brendan. She has long been one of the most popular saints in Ireland.

Jadwiga (1373-1399) was Queen of Poland. She was married to the formerly pagan Władysław of Lithuania, who became a Christian under the terms of the marriage contract and whose lands were thus united to those of Poland. She sponsored writers and artists, encouraged education, and founded hospitals, dispersing much of her own fortune in so doing. Her restoration of the Krakow Academy resulted in its establishment as the Jagiellonian University, one of the most important centres of education in Europe. A cross before which Jadwiga used to pray – and from where Christ is said to have spoken to her – is still venerated there.

Joan/Jane/Joanna/Johanna/Jayne/Joanne is the feminine form of John, and many saints have carried this name. Perhaps the best known is **Joan of Arc** (1412-1421) who, following a vision from Heaven, led an army to drive an

English army out of France and crown the rightful king at Rheims cathedral. She was burned at the stake as a witch but later was affirmed as a saint. St **Jane Frances de Chantal** (1572-1641) was a widow who founded an order of nuns, the Visitation sisters, working with St Francis de Sales. The Order was something entirely new at the time, offering an opportunity for religious life for women who, because of health or other reasons, could not live in the often hard physical conditions of some convents. Jane Frances aimed to encourage women to live entirely according the God's will, with cheerfulness and goodwill.

Kinga/Cunegunda (1224-1292) was the daughter of the King of Hungary and married the Prince of Krakow. This was an arranged marriage and she had always wanted to live as a nun. She and her husband agreed to live as brother and sister and she devoted her life to the care of the poor and sick. After he died she joined the Poor Clares, giving away all her possessions to the needy.

Lourdes is the town in France, where in 1858 St **Bernadette** had a vision of Our Lady. The healing spring there had drawn millions of pilgrims ever since, and it is one of the great Christian centres of prayer and devotion in the world. Bernadette entered a convent and died young: her name, originally a family diminutive of Bernarde, is now a popular girls' name.

Lucy/Lucie/Lucia (d.304) was an early Sicilian martyr and her name means "light". Her feast-day is December 13th and she is popular in Scandinavia where this midwinter feast-day comes in the very darkest time of the year. There are various accounts of her martyrdom: she is said to have died in defence of her virginity and in some versions of the story she was blinded before being killed. She is patron saint of blind people and of young girls.

Madeleine/Magdalene (1st century) was one of Christ's best-known disciples. She stood at the foot of the Cross as he suffered and died, and was the first to see him after his Resurrection. She is often identified with the penitent woman who knelt at Christ's feet and washed them, drying them with her hair. Legend says that she later went to France and lived there as a contemplative in a cave, dedicating herself to prayer.

Margaret (Marguerite/Margery/Marjorie/Meg/Maggie/ Peggy) is the name of a great many saints. The first is said to have been an early Roman martyr but nothing is known about her. **Margaret of Scotland** (1045-1093) was an Anglo-Saxon princess who married Malcolm Canmore, king of Scotland and established the Catholic faith and culture in the kingdom. The towns of North and South Queensferry in Scotland are named after her. **Margaret Clitheroe** (1556-1596) known as the "Pearl of York" was executed for sheltering a priest in the days when the Catholic faith was banned in England. **Marguerite-Marie Alacoque** (1647-1690) was a visionary who popularised devotion to the Sacred Heart of Jesus.

Martha (1st century) lived with her sister Mary (who is sometimes identified as being Mary Magdalene) and their brother Lazarus at Bethany, a house where Christ often visited and where he felt at home. She is described as being busy about the house, cooking and serving the meal and has been hailed as the patron saint of all cooks and housekeepers. She and her sister Mary witnessed Christ raising their brother Lazarus from the dead.

Mary/Marie/Maria/Moira (1st century) is the most important of all female names for Christians. The Gospel of Luke describes how an angel came to the young virgin Mary and told her she was to be the mother of the Saviour. Mary's acceptance allowed the Incarnation to take place, the intervention of God in human history. Literally millions of girls have been named in Mary's honour down the centuries. Among the many saints bearing this name are St **Mary McKillop** (1842-1909) the first Australian-born saint, who established an order of nuns running schools for children in the bush territories, Bl **Mary Restituta Kafka** (1894-1943) who was beheaded by the Nazis after defying an order to remove crucifixes from a hospital where she was working, St **Maria Goretti**, (1890-1902) who was murdered defending her virginity and refusing a young man's sexual advances, and several of the Chinese Martyrs of the "Boxer rebellion" period (1900) including Saint **Mary Fu Guilin**, Saint **Mary Qi Yu**, Saint **Maria Zheng Xu** and St **Mary Hermina Grivot**, who was a missionary sister from France.

Matilda (895-968) married King Heinrich of Germany. She deliberately lived as simply as possible, with few luxuries. She founded several Benedictine monasteries, and used her funds for projects for the poor. After her husband's death, she gave the Church all her jewels. Caught up in disputes between two of her sons, Otto and Henry, she suffered and was badly hurt and betrayed, but bore this without complaint. Another son, Bruno, became Archbishop of Cologne and is hailed as a saint.

Mildred (d.700) joined a convent at Minster-in-Thanet, in Kent, under the guidance of St Theodore, Archbishop of Canterbury. Mildred belonged to the Royal family of Kent, and was educated in France. Her decision to enter a convent was not an easy one and involved turning down a good offer of marriage. She devoted herself to care of the poor and sick, and in due course became abbess at Minster where she was greatly loved by the local people. The Abbey thrives today, and is named in honour of St Mildred.

Monica (337-387) was the mother of St Augustine of Hippo. She had a difficult marriage and the children were not baptised. She was anguished at Augustine's waywardness and prayed much for him: a bishop told her that "it is impossible that the child of so many tears should perish" and in due course he converted and became one of the greatest of Christian writers and teachers whose works are still studied today.

Olivia/Olive (9th century) is said to have been a girl of noble family in Sicily, captured by Islamic pirates in the 9th century and taken to Tunisia. She was forced to be a slave but converted many people by her holiness, courage and faith. Tortured, she refused to renounce Christ and was finally beheaded. The name Olive of course also honours the olive tree - mentioned repeatedly in the Bible - the oil of which is used in sacramental anointing.

Patricia (Tricia/Trixie) is the feminine form of **Patrick**, the famous apostle of Ireland (see below). **Patricia of Naples** (d.c.600) was a Christian in Rome, said to have been related to the Emperor Constantine. She became a nun, renouncing all claims to the throne, and went on a pilgrimage to Jerusalem, but was shipwrecked and died of disease on an island off the shore of Naples.

Pauline/Paulette/Paula/Paola are the feminine form of Paul (see below).

Perpetua (d.203) was an early martyr. She was the mother of small baby when she was condemned to death as a Christian by the pagan authorities. Her servant Felicity, also a Christian, was prepared to die alongside her. Perpetua was allowed to keep her baby with her in prison so that she could feed him – however the authorities also used the baby as a means of trying to persuade her to renounce her faith, which she refused to do.

Petronella (Petronilla/Perronelle) (unknown date) is said to have been an early Christian who was converted by St Peter, hence her name, taken in baptism to honour him. She was later martyred and her remains are with those of other early martyrs beneath St Peter's in Rome.

Priscilla/Prisca (1st century) is mentioned in the Acts of the Apostles, along with her husband Aquila. They were Jewish tent-makers, and they gave hospitality to St Paul on his missionary journey to Corinth. Tradition says they were both later martyred.

Rita (1381-1457) had a difficult marriage. Her patience and gentleness eventually converted her husband and their home became a happy one where they raised their two sons as Christians, but he was later murdered by some old enemies. The two sons pledged to seek revenge and made plans to do so, but Rita prayed that they would fail and both died young of natural causes. Rita entered a convent where she continued to suffer because of a mysterious head wound which kept people away from her. She is the patron saint of problems which appear hopeless.

Rose (1586-1617) was born in Peru. She was very beautiful and her parents were angry when she refused marriage as she wanted to devote her life entirely to Christ – eventually her father allowed her a room of her own at home where she lived as a nun. She made beautiful embroidered lace goods which she sold to give funds to the poor, spent her nights in prayer, lived a harsh life of penance and was widely loved by all the local people, who hailed her as a saint when she died at the age of 31.

Scholastica (c.480-c.583) was the twin sister of St Benedict, founder of the great monastic tradition creating monasteries as we know them today. Her convent was not far from her brother's monastery and they were good friends, although the strict rule meant that they could not often meet. On her last visit to him, they wanted to go on talking together, and in answer to St Scholastica's prayers God sent a great storm which prevented her journeying home for several hours.

Sophia/Sophie/Sofi (dates unknown) – the name means "wisdom" in Greek. There may have been an early Roman martyr named Sophia – she is said to have been a widow with three daughters named Faith, Hope and Charity - but the real importance of the name lies in honouring wisdom and knowledge of great and holy things. "Holy Wisdom", *Hagia Sophia* in Greek, is both a title of Christ and the name of the greatest church in the Christian East, in what is now Istanbul.

Tatiana (dates unknown, 3rd century) was the daughter of a civil servant in the Roman Empire and was brought up as a Christian. As a young adult she was active in the Church and was arrested by the pagan authorities and sentenced to be killed by wild beasts in the arena. It is said that when a lion was set to leap upon her, it instead knelt at her feet. She was later beheaded. St Tatiana is the patron saint of students.

Teresa/Thérèse: Many saints carry this name. Choose from St **Teresa of Avila** (1515-1582) mystic, Doctor of the Church, and reformer of the Carmelite Order, or St **Thérèse of Lisieux** (1873-1897) Doctor of the Church who taught us the "little way" of being Christian living quietly and prayerfully in a Carmelite convent and enduring the trials of life including a painful illness with courage and faith, or Blessed **Teresa of Calcutta** (1910-1997) who founded homes for the destitute and dying, working for the "poorest of the poor" in the slums of the world.

Ursula (dates unknown, maybe 4th century) Little is known for sure of her life. Later legend says she was a Romano-British Christian princess who was betrothed to a pagan German prince. She sailed to meet him accompanied by a large number of bridesmaids, but on discovering that she would have to renounce her faith to marry him, she refused and was martyred along with all the girls accompanying her. She is patron saint of the city of Cologne.

Valerie/Valeria (dates unknown) is a popular French saint, said to have been martyred near Limoges in the Roman era. The story is that she was beheaded, but then miraculously walked, carrying her own head, to the bishop who had originally converted her, to thank him for the gift of the faith, before finally dying at his feet. Another St Valeria, of Milan, is also a martyr of the early centuries, arrested and executed by the pagan Roman authorities for arranging Christian burials.

Veronica (1st century) is the name given to a woman who, according to a very long-held tradition, was moved by pity to wipe the face of Christ as he was carrying the Cross to Calvary. An image of his face was left on the cloth. The name Veronica means "true image".

Winefride (Winifred/Winifride/Gwenffrewi) (d.c.660) was a British martyr. Legend says she was the daughter of a Welsh nobleman who wanted to consecrate her life entirely to God as a nun, and a suitor, Caradoc, was so enraged at this that he attacked and murdered her. A well sprang up at the site of her martyrdom and its waters were said to have healing powers: it is still visited by pilgrims today.

Yvette (Jutta) (1158-1228) was a mystic who was never formally canonised but is widely regarded as a saint in Belgium and Holland where there is much local devotion to her. She was born near Liège, was married while still young and had a large family but was left a widow when not yet twenty. She devoted her life to prayer and penance and succeeded in bring back to the faith members of her family who had left the Church.

Zita (1212-1272) was a serving-maid who lived and worked in Lucca in Tuscany. Often abused and ill-treated by her employers, she responded with courage and quiet faith. Later they came to respect and honour her, and came to a deep religious conversion through her. She worked hard, helped the local poor, was honest and cheerful and prayerful.

Saints' names for boys

Adrian/Hadrian of Canterbury (d.710) was abbot of St Augustine's Abbey at Canterbury and known as a scholar, fluent in Greek and Latin and with a great knowledge of the Scriptures. He was a native of North Africa who accompanied Theodore to Canterbury when the latter was appointed Archbishop there. St **Adrian of May** (9th century) is a Scottish saint, a bishop who established monasteries including one on the island of May: he was martyred by Vikings during a raid in the 9th century.

Alban (3rd century) was the first British martyr. He lived in the days when Britain was part of the Roman Empire. The story is that whilst he sheltered a Christian priest who was hiding from the pagan Roman authorities, he was himself converted and gave himself up in the priest's place. He was executed at Verulamium, where the town of St Albans now stands.

Albert (1193-1280) is sometimes called "Albert the Great" and was a Dominican scholar and Bishop in Germany who emphasised that there is no conflict between science and religious faith. He is a Doctor of the Church.

Andrew (1st century) was one of the Apostles, brother to Peter – they worked as fishermen together. Tradition says that he later died for the Faith, martyred by crucifixion on an X-shaped cross. His relics were brought to Scotland by St **Regulus** or **Rule**, and venerated there: the town of St Andrews commemorates this.

Augustine (Austin) (354-430) was one of the greatest Christian teachers and Bishops of the first centuries of the Church. His writings are still studied today. His conversion to Christianity came after he had sampled other beliefs and ways of living, and his great book *The Confessions*, telling the story of his conversion, has inspired generations. **Augustine of Canterbury** (d.604) was the leader of the missionaries sent from Rome to England in the year 597 – he landed in Kent, made numerous converts including the king, Ethelbert, and was created Archbishop of Canterbury.

Bartholomew (1st century) was one of the twelve Apostles, and is generally identified as being the Nathaniel mentioned in St John's Gospel. Christ said of him "Here is a man in whom there is no deception". St Bartholomew's Hospital in London, known as Barts, was founded in the 12th century in his honour.

Bede (672-735) was a monk at Jarrow in Northumberland and a man of great learning, whose *History of the English*

Church and People is a major source of historical knowledge and one of the most important books produced in Britain. He was declared a Doctor of the Church in 1899, and is the only British-born person so far to have achieved this honour.

Benedict (480-547) was the founder of Western monasticism. The "Rule of St Benedict", dividing the day into times of work, rest and prayer, has guided monks and nuns across the world ever since. He established the first Benedictine community at Monte Cassino in Italy and the Benedictine way of life shaped the way Europe developed, guiding its ideas, its industry, and its farming. He is a patron saint of Europe.

Bernard (1090-1153) founded the great abbey at Clairvaux in France which was known for its austerity and holiness. Huge numbers of men sought to follow him in the Cistercian order. He became a powerful influence in the Church, upholding loyalty to the Pope and preaching against heresy. He is a Doctor of the Church.

Brendan (484-577) known as "the navigator" was an Irish monk and mystic. There are various accounts of a great voyage that he made – it is not clear if it is an allegory or whether or not he really did travel great distances. Some scholars believe that he crossed the Atlantic to America.

He certainly established monastic communities in Wales
and in Scotland – places like Kilbrandon and Kilbrennan
echo his name. He is buried at Clonfert.

Charles (Carlo) (1538-1584) **Borromeo** was a reforming
Archbishop of Milan. Appointed when still only in his
20s, largely through family connections, he proved to be
a formidable opponent of laxity and a hero to the local
people during a time of plague and hardship. Before
his appointment, no archbishop had actually entered
the diocese for 40 years. He visited remote parishes,
and enforced reform of the clergy. **Charles (Karl) of
Austria** (1881-1922) was the last Habsburg Emperor and
sought to bring about social justice and peace, but was
unable to influence events in World War I despite heroic
peace negotiations carried out in the face of danger and
difficulty. He died in poverty and exile, and was beatified
by Pope John Paul in 2004. **Charles Lwanga** was the
leader of the group of boys known as the Ugandan
martyrs, See also **Kizito**.

Clement (d. c98) was the third Pope after St Peter (the
others being Linus and Cletus), and died as a martyr.
A letter from him to the Church at Corinth survives: it
shows that Christians even at that time acknowledged the
authority of the Bishop of Rome. **Clement of Alexandria**
(150-215) was a great scholar of the early Church who

brought insights from the Greek philosophers into Christian thinking. He is a Doctor of the Church.

Cyprian (d.258) was Bishop of Carthage and a noted writer and preacher, many of whose works are still read today. He became a Christian as an adult having, as a pagan, made a distinguished career as a lawyer and orator. He was eventually martyred, being killed in his own villa at Carthage. Bl. **Cyprian Michael Tansi** (1903-1964) was a noted Nigerian priest, born of pagan parents, whose life of dedication and service to the Church had begun with his baptism at the age of nine. As a priest he worked with the poor and with sufferers from leprosy, living personally in great austerity although always cheerful and helpful with everyone. After many years of parish life he became a Cistercian monk at Mount St Bernard in England where he was known for his strict observance of the Rule. He was beatified by John Paul II in 1998.

Damian/Damien (3rd century?) is honoured along with his twin brother **Cosmas** as a martyr. They lived in what is now Turkey, then part of the Roman Empire. According to legend, they were both doctors who gave free medical treatment to anyone who needed it, and were known for their Christian beliefs. Eventually, this brought them into conflict with the pagan Roman authorities. Even under torture, they refused to recant and were executed.

Damien of Molokai (18410-1889) was an heroic missionary priest who lived with leprosy suffers on the island of Molokai and transformed their lives by his love and care. Eventually contracting the disease himself, he was hailed at his death as a "martyr of charity" and is today the patron saint of all suffers from the disease.

David (Dai/Dewi) (500-589) is of course the name of the great king and psalmist of the Old Testament. St David is the patron saint of Wales. He founded a string of monasteries across Wales in which the monks lived a very austere life with no meat and no alcohol. The hill at Llandewi Brefi is said to have sprung up because he was preaching there and needed to be higher up so that everyone could see him. A white dove settled on his shoulder as he preached and this was taken as a sign of the Holy Spirit: he is often depicted with a dove. He is also patron of poets and vegetarians.

Dominic (1170-1221) founded the Order of Preachers, popularly known as the Dominicans. While still a student himself, he sold his books and personal possessions to help the poor at a time of famine in his native Spain. Later, leading his friars, he emphasised personal kindness and holiness while pursuing truth and opposing heresy. He always lived simply, never allowing himself any luxuries or even everyday comforts. He popularised the Rosary, today probably the best-known of all Catholic devotions. Dominicans today preach and teach on every continent.

Dunstan (909-988) was Abbot of Glastonbury in Somerset, a skilled metal worker, a man of scholarship and reading, and a vigorous preacher and organiser. He became Archbishop of Canterbury, restored monastic life in England, which had fallen into disarray, and played a major role in public life through his influence on the king.

Edgar (943-975) was king of England, crowned at Bath where a stone plaque in Bath Abbey still commemorates the event. He unified the country, supported St Dunstan in his efforts at Church reform, and became known as "Edgar the peaceful".

Edmund (c841-869) was king of the Anglo-Saxon kingdom of East Anglia when the Vikings invaded. A devout Christian, after his army was defeated in battle he was offered a treaty which would have kept him in nominal charge of his kingdom if he became a pagan. He refused to renounce his faith and was martyred; the town of Bury St Edmunds commemorates him. **Edmund Campion** (1540-1581) was a brilliant scholar at Oxford, chosen to welcome Queen Elizabeth I on her visit to the university. He became a Jesuit priest and missionary around England at a time when the Catholic faith was banned, was arrested and brutally tortured and suffered martyrdom at Tyburn.

Edward (c.1003-1066) known as "the confessor" was king of England and known for his holy life, and his concern for justice and for the poor. He founded Westminster Abbey on the banks of the Thames which today still has his shrine and is the place where our monarchs are crowned.

Elphege/Alphage (954-1012) was an Anglo-Saxon Archbishop of Canterbury who was martyred by pagan Vikings at Greenwich on the banks of the river Thames. There is a church at Greenwich dedicated to him as well as others in various places, including one at Wallington in Surrey.

Finan (d.656) was an Irish monk on the island of Iona. He was chosen to follow St Aidan as bishop at Lindisfarne, and played a major role in bringing the Christian faith to that part of England. He baptised Peada, the king of the central English kingdom. Finan is said to have been a man of holiness and austerity, who converted people through his sincerity and prayerful life.

Francis (Frank) Francis of Assisi (1181-1226) is one of the most popular of all saints. Born in Umbria into a well-to-do family, he relished parties and adventure, serving for a while as a soldier, and then had a deep conversion experience which led him to renounce all his possessions and serve only Christ. Others joined him, and the Franciscans became known for their joy, their service of the poor, and their loyalty to the Church. Today there are Franciscan friars all over the world. St **Francis de Sales** (1557-1672) was a Bishop who sought the unity of the Church and won back many people who had become involved with extremist Calvinist groups. He emphasised love, kindness, and gentleness, and used pamphlets to put over the Catholic message. His book *An Introduction to the Devout Life* became a classic, and he is the patron saint of writers.

Gabriel is the great Archangel who was sent to bring the news to Mary that she was to be the mother of Christ. He is honoured with the other Archangels, **Michael** and **Raphael**, on September 29th: the feast-day is known as Michaelmas.

George (d. c303) was a martyr in the reign of the Emperor Diocletian. He was a soldier in the Roman Army. According to tradition, when official declarations were made against Christians he joined public opposition: he was arrested and tortured and eventually beheaded. He became a popular saint across the Roman Empire and especially in the Middle East: English soldiers fighting in the Crusades brought back his story to Britain and he is today the patron saint of England. The Polish form of George is Jerzy: **Jerzy Popiełuszko** (1947-1984) was a Polish priest and martyr. Preaching openly about the corruption and cruelty that was part of everyday life under Communism, he posed a threat to the Soviet-backed system and was kidnapped and murdered by secret policemen. His huge following among young people brought thousands of them out on to the streets to mourn him. His message of hope and peace was central in the final non-violent collapse of Communism in Poland. He was beatified as a martyr in 2010.

Gilbert (c.1083-1190) was born at Sempringham in Lincolnshire, the son of the lord of the manor. He studied in Paris, was ordained and founded a number of convents and monasteries in Britain. They were noteworthy because they included both monks and nuns, who lived in separate buildings but had a united rule of prayer and service.

Gregory (c.540-604) known as "the Great" was a scholar and lawyer of an influential Roman family, who became Pope. He reformed the liturgy, was a great administrator of the Church, and is particularly important for England because he sent missionaries here after seeing Anglo-Saxon slaves in a Roman market and wanting to help them become Christians.

Guy/Guido/Wye (c.950-1012) was a poor man who worked as a sacristan in his local church. He saved up his money and invested in some cargo which was to be taken by ship to a great city. However the ship sank and he felt he was being punished for his greed so he set off on a long humble pilgrimage to Rome and then to Jerusalem, befriending and helping hundreds of other pilgrims.

Henry (972-1024) was Holy Roman Emperor and ruled with a sense of Christian service and justice, generous to the Church but honouring its independence, building churches and serving the poor. Many other saints have carried this name including **Henry Morse** (1549-1645) an English martyr who was hanged, drawn and quartered for the crime of being a Catholic priest, **Henry Walpole** (1558-1595) another Catholic martyr who was arrested for being a priest just one day after arriving in England, repeatedly tortured, and finally martyred at Tyburn, and **Henry of Uppsalla**, (d. 1156) who worked to evangelise Scandinavia.

Herbert (d.687) was a hermit who lived on an island that still bears his name at Derwentwater. He was a friend of St Cuthbert and went to visit him once a year for spiritual direction. St Herbert's Island is said to have been the inspiration for Owl Island in Beatrix Potter's *The Tale of Squirrel Nutkin*.

Hilary (Hilaire) (300-368) was born into a pagan family but became a Christian as a young man. He became bishop of Poitiers and was a strong opponent of the Arian heresy. His feast-day is in January and he has thus given his name to the "Hilary term" at Oxford University, the term that begins in that month.

Hubert (658-727) was a missionary who became known as the "Apostle of the Ardennes" and the first Bishop of Liège. He had been married but his wife died in childbirth: he took solace in hunting, but one day he had a sudden vision of the Cross in the antlers of a stag, and heard Christ's voice calling him to change his way of life. He gave away all his goods to the poor, became a priest and dedicated himself to missionary work. He is the patron saint of hunting.

Hugh (1135-1200) was a Carthusian monk and prior of Witham in Somerset, before being appointed Bishop of Lincoln. He became a much-loved and vigorous leader, establishing his independence from the King and government, protecting local Jewish people when a mob set out to attack them, and promoting numerous works of charity and education including the rebuilding of Lincoln Cathedral, which had been damaged in an earthquake. His symbol is a swan, as he had a favourite swan which used to guard him and even watched over him as he slept.

Ignatius – the first known saint of this name was **Ignatius of Antioch**, who died in 108. He was one of the early Church fathers, and from him we learn about the faith of the early Church, as he wrote a series of six letters as he was being taken away to martyrdom. Other saints have had this name down the centuries, the most famous being **Ignatius of Loyola**, (1491-1556), founder of the Jesuits, a former soldier whose *Spiritual Exercises* are still used today and whose vision brought about a renewal of Catholicism in Europe and great missionary work across the world.

James (Jamie/Jim/Jimmy) (d. c.44) was one of the Apostles, brother of St John. He is said to have taken the Gospel to Spain, where he is honoured at the great shrine of Compostela. Pilgrims have for centuries walked to the shrine from different parts of Europe, and the various routes are known as "the way of St James".

Jerome (347-420) was a priest, theologian, and historian. He is most famous for translating the Bible into Latin and thus making it available as a universal book for the Church. He lived in Rome and Bethlehem. His extensive writings are still studied today.

John (Jack/Johnny/Ian/Iain) is one of the best-known names in the history of Christianity. **John the Baptist** was a cousin of Christ, who first greeted him when they were both in the womb, as described in the Gospel of St Luke. The Gospel of **John the Evangelist** is central to our understanding of Christ. Down the centuries, famous saints bearing this name have included **John Chrysostom** (347-407) named the "golden mouthed" because of his wonderful preaching, **John of Avila** (1500-1569) the Spanish preacher and mystic; another Spaniard, **John of the Cross** (1542-1591), Carmelite mystic and poet, and **John Fisher**, Bishop of Rochester, martyred in 1535 on London's Tower Hill on the orders of King Henry VIII.

John Henry Newman (1801-1890) was an Anglican clergyman whose study of the Church Fathers fostered the Tractarian "High Church" Movement in the Church of England in the 1840s. He became a Catholic, established the Oratorians in England and was an influential preacher and writer who drew many to the Church. His hymns including "Praise to the Holiest in the height" are still widely sung today. He was beatified by Pope Benedict XVI in 2010.

John Paul II (1920-2005) was the first-ever Polish Pope and became the most-travelled Pope in history as he went around the world preaching and teaching. He survived an assassination attempt in 1981 and an attempted stabbing a year later, was responsible for popularising devotion to the Divine Mercy, launched World Youth Day which brings together millions of young people from around the world to pray together, brought members of all religions together to pray for peace at Assisi, tirelessly defended human life in opposition to abortion and euthanasia, and became one of the best-loved figures of the 20th century. He was beatified in 2011.

Joseph was the spouse of Mary and foster-father of Christ, and was of the royal line of King David. He protected the Holy Family when they had to flee from Herod and find safety in Egypt. He worked to provide for Mary and the Christ-child, teaching the boy Jesus the trade and skills of carpentry. He is often depicted as an older man, as he was evidently not alive when Christ began his public ministry with his first miracle at Cana in Galilee. He has given his name to many other Josephs down the centuries, such as St **Joseph Benedict Cottolengo** (1786-1842) who founded convents, monasteries, schools and projects for the poor in his native Italy and around the world, and St **Benedict Joseph Labré** (1748-1783), who lived as an impoverished travelling friar, sleeping in hedges and ditches, sharing whatever food he had with the poor, going on pilgrimage, and spending long hours in silent prayer. **Josemaria** Escriva (1902-1975) was founder of the movement Opus Dei which today runs schools, youth centres and various projects around the world.

Justin (c.100-165) is known as Justin Martyr. He was a scholar who became a Christian after first studying Plato and other philosophers. Many of his writings have come down to us. He died for his faith in the reign of Marcus Aurelius after being arrested following a public debate with a pagan philosopher.

Kevin (d.c.618) was the founder of an abbey at Glendalough in Co. Wicklow where there is still a well associated with him. A number of other monasteries were founded from Glendalough. St Kevin is said to have been a mystic and to have lived a penitential life, sleeping at one time on a rough bed on a precipice to which he had been led by an angel.
Kieran/Ciaran (516-546) is one of the "Twelve Apostles of Ireland", monks who established the faith there and made it flourish. He was a learned monk who founded an abbey at Clonmacnois on the Shannon river.

Kitzito (d.1887) was the youngest of the Ugandan martyrs, killed by King Mwanda for affirming their Christian faith and refusing to take part in homosexual activities. These boy-martyrs were all pages at Mwanda's court and were led by St **Charles Lwanga**. Kizito, who was only about 14, was terrified at the thought of being burned alive, but found courage and went to his death joyfully singing the praises of God.

Lawrence/Laurence (Larry) (225-258) – the name means "honoured with laurels", was a deacon in Rome and was martyred in the persecution of the Emperor Valerian. When he was ordered by the Roman authorities to gather together the treasures of the Church he brought together a great group the poor, the handicapped, and the sick and told the authorities "these are the treasures of the Church." He is said to have been martyred by being roasted on a gridiron. There was a chapel of St Lawrence at Westminster, and the "portcullis" logo on Parliamentary notepaper originated with the gridiron of St Lawrence.

Leo (d.461) was a Pope, known as "the great". He defended Rome when it was attacked by Huns, meeting Attila at the gates of the city and persuading him to turn back. Leo did not attend in person the Council of Chalcedon, which had been called to debate the nature of Christ, but sent a letter, known as "Tome of Leo" affirming the full divinity and full humanity of Christ, which decided the issue.

Linus (d. c.76) is thought to have been the next Pope after St Peter. He is probably the Linus mentioned by St Paul in the second letter to Timothy, chapter 4, verse 21.

Louis/Lewis IX (1214-1270) was king of France: he inherited the throne at the age of eleven but his mother acted as regent until he was of full age. He promoted Christianity throughout the kingdom, founded religious institutions, and established hospitals and homes for the poor. He married Marguerite of Provence and they had a large family together. He supported the Crusades and died while *en route* to the Holy Land.

Lucius (d. c. 165) was an early Roman martyr who met his death because he dared to defend another Christian who had been unjustly accused of crime. There is also a semi-legendary **Lucius of Britain**, a king who is said to have played a central role in establishing Christianity in Britain in the last years of Roman rule, and a **Pope St Lucius** (d.254) who was notable for showing mercy and kindness to Christians who sought to rejoin the Church after lapsing from the faith during times of persecution.

Luke (1st century) is one of the four Gospel writers – it is from him that we get the account of the visit of Gabriel to Mary telling her she was to be the mother of the Saviour, and of Christ's birth at Bethlehem. He was a Greek, and also wrote the Acts of the Apostles, describing the first days of the early Church and the great missionary journeys of St Paul.

Magnus (d.1075) was a ruler of Orkney – jointly with his brother Paul - and a Christian Viking. He is said to have been kidnapped by the king of Norway and forced into piracy, which he resisted, staying on the ship and singing hymns instead. Later, after returning home, and taking up his responsibilities as ruler or Orkney, he was treacherously killed on the orders of a cousin.

Martin (316-397) was a soldier in the Roman Army. Legend says that he saw a beggar shivering with cold one night and slashed his uniform cloak in half so that he could share it with him. He became a priest and in due course Bishop of Tours: he defended the faith against the Arian heresy and against the inroads of paganism. Devotion to him became strong in France in the 19th century as a figure around whom French patriots could rally: he is also popular in Hungary and in Poland. **Martin de Porres** (1579-1639) was a lay brother of the Dominican order. He was born illegitimate, the son of a nobleman and a former slave, and is patron saint of mixed-race children and victims of racial prejudice. He worked with the poor and homeless, and had miraculous gifts including healing and being able to talk to animals: it is said he once politely asked some mice to leave a building, and they did.

Maximilian Kolbe (1894-1941) was a Franciscan friar who became known for his work in publishing Catholic papers and magazines. Arrested by the Nazis in occupied Poland, he was sent to Auschwitz. When the camp authorities randomly selected some prisoners to die by slow starvation in an underground bunker, St Maximilian stepped forward to take the place of one of them, and died as a "martyr of charity", He was canonised in 1982.

Milo (d.1057) was archbishop of Benevento in Italy, known for his inspiring preaching. A noble family were visiting the city when their son became seriously ill. Archbishop Milo took charge of the boy and he recovered, later going on to become a saint, St **Stephen of Muret**, and the founder of a religious order.

Nicholas (Niklaus/Claus/Nick/Nicky) (270-343) was an early Bishop of the Church who defended the full divinity of Christ against the Arian heresy, was generous to the poor and worked for the moral welfare of children and young people. His feast-day on December 6th has linked him with Christmas giving us the figure of Santa Claus. **Nicholas von Flue** (1417-1487) was a Swiss hermit and mystic, a former soldier who became a farmer, married and had a large family but with their consent left them to live alone. He was much valued for his wisdom and his counsel to local leaders prevented a civil war – he is regarded as the saint of Switzerland's unity.

Norbert (1080-1184) founded the religious order known as the Premonstratensians (after Prémontré, where he built a small abbey which was initially just a collection of huts around a chapel) or Norbertines. They worked as preachers and still flourish today. Norbert preached against heresy, lived an austere and simple life, supported the Pope in various controversies, and helped the Church flourish in France, Germany and the Low Countries. He is buried at Magdeburg.

Olaf/Olave (995-1030) was king of Norway. Baptised in Rouen in France during early travels, he played a major role in establishing Christianity in Norway, bringing in missionary bishops from England, Normandy, and Germany. He battled to unify the country against various enemies and is Norway's patron saint.

Oliver Plunket (1629-1681) was Bishop of Armagh during the time of persecution of the Catholic faith. He was arrested and brought to London for trial: he was not allowed time to state his defence or bring witnesses from Ireland, and a jury took just fifteen minutes to convict him of treason. He was hanged, drawn and quartered at Tyburn, the last Catholic martyr to die for the faith in this way in England. The first St **Oliver** (d.1050) was a monk in Italy of whom little is known.

Patrick (c.387-c.490) was a Romano-Briton who was captured while a young man living in what we now call England, and taken to Ireland. He worked there herding animals but after some years was able to escape and make his way home. He became a priest and returned to Ireland as a missionary. He is said to have banished all the snakes from Ireland, and to have used the little shamrock plant to illustrate the Holy Trinity.

Paul (d. c.65) He was the great missionary of the early Church, a former persecutor of Christians who was converted dramatically while travelling to Damascus, as described in the Acts of the Apostles. He took the Gospel to the lands around the Mediterranean including Greece, Malta, Syria and Turkey, and established churches around the Middle East and the Mediterranean. His letters to them are still read today and form part of the New Testament. He has given his name to many other saints over the years including **Paul of the Cross** (1694-1695) who founded the Passionist order devoted to prayer, solitude, and preaching.

Peter (first century) was the leader of the Apostles. There are more mentions of him in the Gospels than any other Apostles, and he always acted as spokesman for the others. Christ asked him to "feed my lambs ...feed my sheep" and thus is reckoned to have appointed him the first Pope. He went to Rome, where he was martyred – tradition says by being crucified upside down as he did not feel worthy to die as his Master had done. Among the many saints named after him are St **Peter Canisius** (1521-1597) who worked to bring the reforms and teachings of the Council of Trent to Christians in Germany and elsewhere, writing a Catechism for the purpose, and St **Peter Claver** (1580-1654) who worked to alleviate the sufferings of African slaves taken to America, and taught them the Gospel.

Petroc/Perreux (d.564) was a missionary, born in Wales, who worked in Devon, Cornwall, and Somerset and in Brittany. He established a monastery at Padstow and one at Bodmin and there are churches and places named in his honour across the West Country of Britain.

Philip (Felipe/Phillipe) (first century) was an Apostle and is mentioned several times in the New Testament, notably at the Last Supper where he asks Christ about the Father. He came from Bethsaida and his name is Greek so he may have been Greek-speaking. There have been a number of other St Philips, notably St **Philip Howard**, (1557-1595), Earl of Arundel, who died in the Tower of London for refusing to renounce his Catholic faith in the days when being a Catholic meant being accused of treason, and **Philip Neri** (1515-1595), founder of the Oratorians and "Apostle of Rome".

St **Pio (Pius)** (1887-1968) known as "Padre Pio", was a Franciscan mystic who carried the stigmata, and attracted thousands of pilgrims to the church where he served at Pietrelcina in Italy. He bore with patience many calumnies against him and became a much-loved spiritual director, urging daily prayer and weekly confession – which he compared to cleaning a room regularly – and giving the simple advice "Pray, hope, and don't worry". Various Popes have also carried the name Pius and been canonised or beatified, notably Pius V, IX and X.

Polycarp (c99-155) was Bishop of Smyrna and a martyr. He is one of the early Fathers of the Church and a direct link with the Apostles, as he is said when a young man to have listened to St John preaching.

Quentin/Quintin (unknown date) is an early martyr of the Roman Empire, associated with Amiens in France. He is said to have been tortured and then thrown into the Somme river.

Raymond – There are several saints with this name, one (d.1240) is known as "nonnatus" because he was delivered by Caesarian section after his mother died trying to give birth to him. He became a monk and went to Algeria to plead for Christians who had been captured and taken there as slaves. He converted several Muslims and is said to have been tortured by having his lips burned so that he could no longer preach. Another, **Raymond of Penyafort** (c1180-1275), was a Spanish Dominican expert in Canon Law who fostered the study of Arabic and Hebrew and encouraged Thomas Aquinas to write his great *Summa contra Gentiles*. He is a patron of lawyers. **Raymond Palmerio** of Piacenza (1140-1200) was a layman known for heroic works of charity to the poor and sick.

Reginald (d.1290) was a Dominican, the friend and confessor of St Thomas Aquinas, and a much-loved teacher and preacher in his own right.

Richard of Chichester (1197-1253) was born at Wych (now Droitwich) in Worcestershire, to the family of the manor there. He studied in Oxford and Paris and was ordained. He studied with the Dominicans, became Bishop of Chichester and was known for his austere life and his dedication to his people.

Rupert (660-710) was a missionary bishop in at Regensburg in Bavaria and the founder of the city of Salzburg in Austria. He converted large numbers of people all along the river Danube, and founded schemes of education and systems for the relief of the poor. **Robert/Robin/Bob** is a name carried by several saints. **Robert Southwell** (1561-1595) was a priest, poet and martyr who ministered secretly to Catholics in England in the days when the Catholic faith was banned. He was captured and viciously tortured, being left in agony, covered in lice, in a dungeon in his own filth. He was finally hanged, drawn and quartered at Tyburn.

Sebastian (d. c300) was a Roman martyr in the reign of Diocletian. The story is that he was a soldier who defended other Christians in the Roman Army and then publicly affirmed his own faith. Denounced by Diocletian as a traitor to the Empire, he is said to have met his death by being tied to a stake and shot with arrows.

Simon (1st century) was the original name of the man who became leader of the Apostles. He was a fisherman, and Christ called him and gave him a new name: see **Peter**. **St Simon Stock** (1165-1265) was a Carmelite priest, prior at Aylesford in Kent, who was once said to have received a vision of Our Lady who gave him the Carmelite habit of the Brown Scapular. Small versions of the scapular have for centuries been blessed and worn as a popular devotion.

Sixtus (d. 258) was an early Pope who was a martyr, dying for the faith in Rome during the persecution of the Emperor Valerian. He is mentioned in the Canon of the Mass. He was the second Pope to have the name Sixtus: the first is also a saint, although not a martyr: **Sixtus I**, who issued various rules about Bishops and about the liturgy, stating that the priest and people should say the Sanctus together, as we still do today, and that Bishops should not be received by their dioceses unless they have letters from Rome confirming their appointment.

Stanislaus (Stanisław) (1013-1079) was Bishop of Krakow in Poland. After a dispute with the King Bolesław, he was martyred – killed by the king himself after various soldiers refused to do the deed. He is a patron saint of Poland along with Adalbert of Prague, St Florian and Our Lady Queen of Poland. **Stanislaus Koska** (1550-1568) was a young Jesuit novice and mystic, who died young and was noted for his spirit of charity, penance, and devotion.

Stephen was the first Christian martyr, and his death is described in the Acts of the Apostles. The mob that stoned him to death laid their cloaks at the foot of a man named Saul who would later be dramatically converted and be known as St **Paul**. Stephen would give his name to other saints down the centuries, including St **Stephen of Hungary** (d.1038) who was the first king of that country and established its Christian identity. The name Stephen means "crown".

Swithun/Swithin (d. 862) was a Bishop of Winchester who lived a humble and hard-working life, known for his zeal in building up local churches and communities. After his death he was buried at Winchester: he had wanted a very simple grave but his remains were later moved into a grand one. He is associated with a tradition which says that the weather on his feast-day (July 15th) will continue for forty days – because God sent rain for forty days to mark displeasure at the way in which Swithun's wishes about his burial-place were ignored. **Swithun Wells** (1536-1591) was an English martyr, a layman, who refused to renounce his Catholic faith during the days when the Mass was outlawed: he was executed outside his own house, along with a priest, St Edward Gennings, and was canonised in 1970.

Tarcissius (3rd century) Legend says that he was a 12-year-old boy in the days of pagan Rome who was on his way taking Holy Communion to a sick person when he was set upon by youths. They were boys of his own age who wanted to know why he would not join in their sports as he usually did: unwilling to reveal the secret of the Eucharist he remained silent and when they attacked him he tried to protect the Blessed Sacrament and did not fight back. He later died of his injuries.

Thomas was one of the Apostles, best known for this affirmation "My Lord and my God" on finally meeting the risen Christ: he had not been present when the Apostles first knew of the Resurrection and had doubted its possibility. He became a great missionary and is said to have taken the Gospel to India, where he is still much honoured. Many Christian men have had this name in the centuries since, and famous saints include **Thomas Becket** (1118-1170) Archbishop of Canterbury martyred in his own cathedral after a dispute with the king, and **Thomas More** (d. 1535),

Chancellor of England, who was martyred on the orders of King Henry VIII for refusing to acknowledge the king as head of the Church.

Titus (first century) was a companion of St Paul and is mentioned in several of the Epistles, travelling to Ephesus and Corinth. He was a vigorous missionary and teacher and is said to have been appointed a Bishop in Crete, establishing a strong Christian community there.

Urban (d.230) was an early Pope. Little is known about him, but we do know for certain that he reigned from 222 to 230. It was a peaceful time when there was no persecution of Christians and, unusually for an early Pope, Urban seems to have died of natural causes.

Valentine (3rd century) is said to have been an early Roman martyr, perhaps a priest who, legend has it, preached about true Christian love and the importance of marriage.

Victor (d.303) was a Christian Roman soldier, known as Victor Maurus or Victor the Moor, who served in the Praetorian Guard near what is now Milan in Italy. After destroying some altars to pagan idols, he was arrested, tortured, and killed. There was also a Victor (d. c199) who was Pope and died as a martyr, but little is known about him.

Vincent (d.304) was a deacon, born at Saragossa in Spain. He was a martyr under the Emperor Diocletian, and is aid to have been tortured by, among other things, scourging and being imprisoned in a cell strewn with broken pots so he could not lie down and sleep. St **Vincent de Paul** (1581-1660) was a priest who dedicated his life to the service of the poor; and has given his name to a major Catholic charity devoted to this, which still carries on the work today.

Wilfred (Wilfrid/Wilfrith) (c.633-709) was an English Bishop. He had studied at Lindisfarne and became Abbot at Ripon. He supported the Roman side in debates at the Synod of Whitby, became Bishop of Northumbria, and was caught up in dispute which resulted in his being exiled for some years to Sussex, where he converted many of the local pagan Saxons.

William/Will/Bill/Billy (d.1154) was an Archbishop of York who carried out a number of reforms and was popular locally, but suffered much from political machinations that resulted in his being deprived of his diocese. When he finally returned to York there was great jubilation, but he died only a month later, it is said by poisoning. Miracles began to be associated with him very shortly after his death and his tomb at York became a place of pilgrimage.

Yves/Ives/Ivo (1253-1303) was born in Brittany and studied law in Paris. Working as an official for the Bishop of Treguier, he opposed unjust taxes and worked to help poor people suffering legal difficulties. He later became a priest. He is another patron saint of lawyers.

Has this book helped you?
Spread the word!

@CTSpublishers

/CTSpublishers

ctscatholiccompass.org

Let us know!
marketing@ctsbooks.org
+44 (0)207 640 0042

Learn, love, live your faith.
www.CTSbooks.org